Sustainability Guidelines

2010 Edition

CMAA

**Advancing Professional Construction/
Program Management Worldwide**

Cover image: National Petascale Computing Facility
2010 CMAA Project Achievement Award
Owner is the National Center for Supercomputing
Applications of the University of Illinois
CM is Clayco, Inc.
LEED® Gold certification
Photo courtesy of Matthew McFarland

7926 Jones Branch Drive, Suite 800
McLean, VA 22102-3303 USA
703.356.2622   703.356.6388 fax
www.cmaanet.org

Acknowledgements

Without the expertise and time from members of the CMAA Sustainability Committee, this valuable resource would not exist. CMAA is grateful for the efforts from the following:

Lonnie Coplen, LEED AP, Jacobs Engineering, New York, NY

Jennifer Creighton, LEED AP, McKinstry | Energy & Facility Solutions, Seattle, WA

Joyce Dawson, CCM, LEED AP, Anne Arundel Community College, Arnold, MD

Juan Giron, PE, LEED, City of Phoenix, Phoenix, AZ

Lourdes Gonzalez, AIA, LEED AP, Primera, Chicago, IL

Don Green, CCM, CCC, LEED AP, Heery International, Inc., Atlanta, GA

Judith Kunoff, AIA, CCM, LEED AP, MTA NYCT, New York, NY

Don Laford, PE, CCM, URS Corporation, Seattle, WA

Christopher Magent, PhD, LEED AP, Alexander Building Construction, State College, PA

Mickey Rosenblum, CCM, Knoxville, TN

Ron Whisker, CCM, LEED AP, Harrisburg, PA

Table of Contents

1.0 Introduction and Definitions

1.1 Introduction

The intention of the Sustainability Guidelines is to provide the CM a starting point for implementing a "sustainable," "green," or "high-performance" project. The Sustainability Guidelines does not offer a prescriptive approach designed to yield a sustainable project; it offers information and guidance on the application of CM tools and processes to yield a sustainable project.

The most critical step in producing a sustainable project is the owner's adoption of sustainability as a guiding principle of design. Thereafter, consistent application of project and construction management practices, meticulous documentation, common sense, and good engineering is likely to yield a sustainable project.

The Sustainability Guidelines provides for the integration of sustainability with other functions integral to the practice of Construction Management, and identifies key management measures and opportunities in each phase of the project life cycle. To successfully implement a project with sustainability objectives or features, the practitioner must be cognizant of a CM's key responsibilities with respect to the sustainability program:

- As a professional, the CM is responsible for maintaining a current understanding of the changing regulatory environment, emerging best practices, and rapidly evolving technological improvements in energy and ecological high performance, monitoring, measurement and control technologies.

- As the owner's agent, the CM is responsible for educating the owner and the project team on the benefits, features, limitations and the implementation processes of a project's sustainability features.

- As the team leader, the CM is responsible for encouraging an environment of learning and exploration regarding the application of CM best practices at the service of achieving sustainability on a project.

- As a CM-at-Risk, the CM is responsible for assembling a team of subcontractors and consultants who are aware of and committed to building a sustainable project that conforms to the commitment of the owner.

If the definition of a sustainable project is a project that provides a conveyance, shelter or production functionality in a manner that conserves natural resources, protects the natural environment and sustains the community, then sustainability

1

objectives are met with the successful implementation of CM best practices on a project that has sustainability as a guiding design principle.

1.1.1 Sustainability objectives

The primary objectives of sustainable design are to avoid resource depletion of energy, water, and raw materials; prevent environmental degradation throughout the facility life cycle; and to produce well constructed environments that are livable, comfortable, safe, and productive.

Thus, common features of a sustainable project include:

- Water conservation and management systems;
- Energy conservation measures or features;
- Renewable energy systems and applications;
- Sustainably derived materials;
- Waste minimization plans; and
- Systems designed to assure healthy indoor environments by minimizing contaminants during construction and operations.

Strategies to achieve sustainability objectives include:

- Optimization of site/existing structure potential;
- Optimization of energy use;
- Protection/conservation of water;
- Use of "environmentally preferable products";
- Enhancement of indoor air quality; and
- Optimization of operational and maintenance procedures.

Achieving the objectives of a sustainable project requires applying a process intended to yield a sustainable design, and the implementation of construction and assembly practices intended to yield a facility that has sustainability features.

1.2 Definitions

Acceptance testing
When a full commissioning program is not justified, specific pieces of equipment or systems can be subject to "acceptance testing" for purposes of owner acceptance. Acceptance testing requirements are clearly identified in contract documents. Training owner personnel in operation and maintenance is part of the acceptance test.

AIA
American Institute of Architects, a professional membership and advocacy association for "licensed architects, emerging professionals and allied partners."

Reference:
- American Institute of Architects: http://www.aia.org/index.htm

AGC

The Associated General Contractors of America, a membership advocacy organization comprising thousands of construction contractors, service providers and suppliers.

Reference:
- American General Contractors of America: http://www.agc.org/

ASHRAE

American Society of Heating, Refrigerating, and Air-Conditioning Engineers, founded in 1894. ASHRAE's mission is to advance "heating, ventilation, air conditioning and refrigeration to serve humanity and promote a sustainable world through research, standards writing, publishing and continuing education." ASHRAE offers definitive guidance on energy load calculations, equipment performance, commissioning and many other topics central to design, engineering and construction of sustainable facilities.

Reference:
- ASHRAE: http://www.ashrae.org/

Building commissioning

Startup, calibration and certification of a facility. This activity or group of activities involves testing and verification of HVAC and other systems against design intent or criteria. Commissioning also may include preparation of the system operation manuals and instruction of the building maintenance personnel. See "Commissioning."

C&D waste management

Construction and demolition (C&D) waste or debris is defined as that part of the solid waste stream that results from land clearing and excavation, and the construction, demolition, remodeling and repair of structures, roads and utilities. Nationwide, C&D debris accounts for 25 percent to 45 percent of the total solid waste stream (by weight), with the balance consisting of regular municipal and commercial trash. Management strategies include waste prevention, waste reduction, recycling and re-use.

Carbon footprint

The overall volume, over a specified period, of greenhouse gas (GHG) emissions caused by an organization, event or product. While it is often expressed in terms of the carbon dioxide for the sake of simplicity, atmospheric carbon has several physical manifestations (e.g., methane), and carbon footprint can correlate positively with activities or processes that curtail the earth's natural GHG management or sequestration capacity, such as deforestation and rising sea temperatures. The carbon footprint is a subset of the ecological footprint and is a factor in the Life Cycle Assessment (LCA).

Commissioning

ASHRAE defines commissioning as "a quality-oriented process for achieving, verifying, and documenting that the performance of facilities, systems, and assemblies meets defined objectives and criteria." According to the National Institute of Building Sciences, commissioning is "an all inclusive process for all the planning, delivery, verification, and managing risks to critical functions performed in, or by,

3

facilities." Commissioning is intended to improve building quality via peer review and in-field or on-site verification and heighten energy efficiency, environmental performance and occupant safety. Commissioning can improve indoor air quality by making sure building components work correctly. It provides a system for documenting project implementation as a function of design intent. Commissioning is a quality assurance-based process that utilizes preventive and predictive maintenance plans, tailored operating manuals and training procedures for all users to follow. From a life cycle perspective, the commissioning process formalizes review and integration of all project expectations throughout planning, design, construction, and occupancy phases via periodic (planned) inspections and functional performance testing, and oversight of operator training and documentation.

Some government agencies, including GSA, NAVFAC, and USACE, have adopted formal requirements, standards or criteria for commissioning of their capital construction projects. However, the extent of commissioning utilized will depend on project funds available.

References:
- AIA: AIA B211™—2004 Standard Form of Architect's Services: Commissioning
- ASHRAE: ASHRAE Guideline 0 - 2005: The Commissioning Process
- U.S. General Services Administration: The Building Commissioning Guide, http://www.wbdg.org/ccb/browse_doc.php?d=5434
- Building Commissioning Association: http://www.bcxa.org/resources/pubs/index.htm
- The National Institute of Building Sciences: http://www.wbdg.org/project/buildingcomm.php

Commissioning Agent (CA)
The Commissioning Agent is responsible for developing and coordinating the execution of the Commissioning Plan, and for observation and documentation of performance—that is, determining whether systems are functioning in accordance with the documented design intent and in accordance with the contract documents. The CA is not responsible for design concept, design criteria, compliance with codes, design or general construction scheduling, cost estimating, or construction management. (Commissioning Agent is often synonymous with Commissioning Authority.) The CA should be an independent, third party consultant that is directly accountable to the owner.

Credentials for commissioning professionals are offered by ASHRAE and the Building Commissioning Association.

References:
- ASHRAE: http://www.ashrae.org/certification/page/2086
- Building Commissioning Association: http://www.bcxa.org/certification/index.htm

Contingency
Contingency is an amount of money reserved by a party for unforeseen changes in the work or increases in cost.

ConsensusDOCS green building addendum

ConsensusDOCS™ is a coalition of associations representing diverse interests in the construction industry that collaboratively develops and promotes standard form construction contract documents that advance the construction process. The organization's new ConsensusDOCS 310 Green Building Addendum is designed to allocate risk and to clarify roles and responsibilities on a sustainable building project.

Reference:
- AGC ConsensusDOCS 310 Green Building Addendum

Deconstruction (building)
Selective dismantling of building components specifically for C&D waste management strategies such as re-use and recycling. Deconstruction differs from demolition, which values the expedient clearing of a building from its site above C&D re-use and recycling objectives.

Energy service company (ESCO)
A business that develops, installs, and arranges financing for projects designed to improve the energy efficiency and maintenance costs for facilities over a seven to 20-year time period. ESCOs generally act as project developers for a wide range of tasks and assume the technical and performance risk associated with the project in exchange for repayment through the value of the energy savings generated by the project.

Energy Star
A joint program of the U.S. Environmental Protection Agency (EPA) and the U.S. Department of Energy introduced in 1992 by the EPA as a voluntary labeling program designed to identify and promote energy-efficient products to reduce greenhouse gas emissions. EPA recently extended the ENERGY STAR label to cover new homes and commercial and industrial buildings.

Reference:
- Energy Star Program: http://www.energystar.gov/

Environmental justice
According to the U.S. Environmental Protection Agency (EPA), environmental justice is the fair treatment and meaningful involvement of all people regardless of race, color, national origin, or income with respect to the development, implementation, and enforcement of environmental laws, regulations, and policies. Environmental justice will be achieved when everyone enjoys the same degree of protection from environmental and health hazards and equal access to the decision-making process to have a healthy environment in which to live, learn, and work.

Reference:
- U.S. EPA, Environmental Justice: http://www.epa.gov/compliance/ej/

Environmentally preferable products
Environmentally-preferable products (EPPs), as defined by the federal government in Executive Order 13101, are those that have "a lesser or reduced effect on human health and the environment when compared to competing products that serve the same purpose."

Reference:
- U.S. EPA Environmentally Preferable Purchasing: http://www.epa.gov/epp/

Green Building Initiative (GBI)

The Green Building Initiative (GBI) is a not-for-profit organization whose mission is to accelerate the adoption of building practices that result in energy-efficient, healthier and environmentally sustainable buildings by promoting credible and practical green building approaches for residential and commercial construction.

Reference:
- GBI: http://www.thegbi.org/

Green Building Facilitator (GBF)

The project team member responsible for facilitating the receipt of information, submittals and other deliverables needed to verify performance of tasks necessary to achieve the project's sustainability objectives. The role of the GBF may be filled by the CM, a member of the CM's staff, an independent Commissioning Agent, or another party whose efforts are monitored by the CM organization.

Reference:
- AGC ConsensusDOCS 310 Green Building Addendum

Green Globes

The Green Building Initiative (GBI) Green Globes is a development and management tool that includes an assessment protocol, a rating system and guide for integrating environmentally friendly design into both new and existing commercial buildings.

Reference:
- GBI: http://www.greenglobes.com/design/homeca.asp

Greenhouse gas (GHG) emissions

Gases that trap heat in the earth's atmosphere. GHGs occur naturally or are generated by human activity. Carbon dioxide (CO_2) enters the atmosphere as a byproduct of combustion of fossil fuels (oil, natural gas, and coal), decomposition of organic matter, mammalian respiration, and other chemical reactions. Carbon dioxide is removed from the atmosphere through absorption by plants. Methane (CH_4) is emitted during the production and transport of coal, natural gas, and oil. Methane emissions also result from livestock and other agricultural practices and by the decay of organic waste in municipal solid waste landfills. Nitrous oxide (N_2O) is emitted during agricultural and industrial activities, as well as during combustion of fossil fuels and solid waste. Fluorinated synthetic gases such as hydrofluorocarbons, perfluorocarbons, and sulfur hexafluoride are powerful GHG byproducts of a variety of industrial processes.

Reference:
- U.S. EPA: http://www.epa.gov/climatechange/emissions/index.html

Greywater system

Greywater is wash water: bath, dish, and laundry water excluding toilet wastes and garbage. A greywater system is designed to assure isolation of greywater collection and treatment from blackwater (sewage), which contains higher concentrations of nitrogen and bacteria.

High performance building
Synonymous with "green" building, a facility that meets environmental impact management objectives.

Integrated Project Delivery
Integrated Project Delivery (IPD) is a delivery system that seeks to align goals, through a team-based approach. The primary team members would include the architect, owner, CM, key technical consultants as well as a general contractor and key subcontractors. The IPD system is a process where all stakeholders in a construction project work as one firm (organization), creating faster delivery times, lower costs, no litigation and a more enjoyable (professional) process for the entire team – including the owner.

References:
- AIA
- AGC

ISO 14000
The International Organization for Standardization (ISO) is a non-governmental organization the world's largest developer and publisher of International Standards. ISO is a network of the national standards institutes of 159 countries, one member per country, with a Central Secretariat in Geneva, Switzerland, that coordinates the system. The U.S. is represented by the American National Standards Institute (ANSI). The ISO 14000 family addresses various aspects of environmental management. The very first two standards, ISO 14001:2004 and ISO 14004:2004 deal with environmental management systems (EMS). ISO 14001:2004 provides the requirements for an EMS and ISO 14004:2004 gives general EMS guidelines. Other ISO 14000 standards and guidelines address issues including labeling, performance evaluation, life cycle analysis, communication and auditing.

Reference:
- International Organization for Standardization: http://www.iso.org/iso/home.html

Leadership in Energy and Environmental Design (LEED®)
The Leadership in Energy and Environmental Design (LEED) Green Building Rating System™ encourages and accelerates global adoption of sustainable green building and development practices through the application of design and construction and a graduated performance-based rating system with four increasingly rigorous levels of attainment: Certified, Silver, Gold and Platinum. LEED is a consensus guideline developed and administered by the U.S. Green Building Council, a non-profit organization.

Reference:
- U.S. Green Building Council: http://www.usgbc.org/DisplayPage.aspx?CategoryID=19

LEED AP

LEED Accredited Professional, the professional credential awarded to an individual that has demonstrated a thorough understanding of the LEED green building rating system by successfully passing the LEED AP examination. The LEED professional credential program is administered by the Green Building Certification Institute, an independent organization that provides third-party certification.

Reference:
- Green Building Certification Institute: http://www.usgbc.org/DisplayPage.aspx?CMSPageID=1815

Life cycle
The consecutive, interlinked stages of a product's production and use, beginning with raw materials acquisition and manufacture and continuing with its fabrication, manufacture, construction, use, and depletion, concluding with any of a variety of recovery, recycling, or waste management options.

Life cycle cost
All costs incident to the planning, design, construction, operation, maintenance and demolition of a facility, or system, for a given life expectancy, all in terms of present value.

Reference:
- NIBS: http://www.wbdg.org/resources/lcca.php

Life Cycle Assessment
LCA is commonly used to evaluate and compare the environmental advantages of products, materials and assemblies. The goal of LCA is to compare the full range of environmental and social damages attributable to the production and use of goods and services in support of decision-making along the product or service delivery pathway. The term "life cycle" refers to the stage of a product or process evolution, including raw material production, manufacture, distribution, use and disposal, and all intermediate or final transition or delivery activities. Common categories of assessed damages are climate change (greenhouse gas emissions), acidification, smog, ozone layer depletion, eutrophication, eco-toxicological and human-toxicological pollutants, habitat destruction, desertification, land use and depletion of non-renewable resources. The four fundamental stages of LCA are goal and scope definition, inventory analysis, impact assessment, and interpretation. The procedures for LCA are part of the ISO 14000 environmental management standards: in ISO 14040:2006 and 14044:2006. (ISO 14044 replaced earlier versions of ISO 14041 to ISO 14043.) The U.S. EPA also offers LCA guidance.

References:
- International Organization for Standardization: http://www.iso.org/iso/catalogue_detail?csnumber=37456
- U.S. EPA: http://www.epa.gov/nrmrl/lcaccess/

National Institute of Building Sciences (NIBS)
A non-profit, non-governmental organization comprising representatives of government, the professions, industry, labor and consumer interests "to focus on the identification and resolution of problems and potential problems that hamper the construction of safe, affordable structures for housing, commerce and industry

throughout the United States. NIBS was authorized by the U.S. Congress in the Housing and Community Development Act of 1974, Public Law 93-383. In establishing the Institute, Congress recognized the need for an organization that could serve as an interface between government and the private sector. The Institute's public interest mission is to support advances in building science and technology to improve the built environment. NIBS' "Whole Building Design Guide" is an authoritative and comprehensive source of information on project management best practices, including commissioning.

Reference:
- National Institute of Building Sciences: http://www.wbdg.org/index.php

Net zero
A "net zero" energy building refers to a facility with zero net energy consumption and zero carbon emissions annually.

Off-the-grid
An off-the-grid building is a stand-alone or autonomous "zero-energy building" that is not connected to an off-site energy utility facility, requiring renewable energy generation and energy storage capabilities.

Rainwater harvesting
Considered a sustainable water management practice, rainwater harvesting is a strategy to divert rainwater for use shortly after precipitation to collection and treatment systems. In urban settings, rainwater harvesting averts water from waste management systems where it is directed by the impervious surfaces of urban infrastructure, and re-directs it for uses that do not require treatment, such as irrigation or flushing sanitary fixtures.

Renewable energy
Energy generated from renewable resources such as sunlight, wind, rain, tides, and some geothermal applications, which are naturally and readily replenished, or renewable.

References:
- U.S. DOE National Renewable Energy Laboratory: http://www.nrel.gov/
- U.S. DOE Energy Efficiency and Renewable Energy: http://www.eere.energy.gov/

Renewable Energy Credits (RECs)
A key element of the carbon cap-and-trade mechanism. Also known as Green tags, Renewable Energy Credits, Renewable Electricity Certificates, or Tradable Renewable Certificates (TRCs), are tradable, non-tangible energy commodities in the U.S. that represent proof that 1 megawatt-hour (MWh) of electricity was generated from an eligible renewable energy resource (renewable electricity). RECs can be sold and traded or bartered, and the owner of the REC can claim to have purchased renewable energy. While traditional carbon emissions trading programs promote low-carbon technologies by increasing the cost of emitting carbon, RECs can incentivize carbon-neutral renewable energy by providing a production subsidy to electricity generated from renewable sources. It is important to understand that the energy associated with a REC is sold separately and is used by another party. The consumer of a REC receives only a certificate. In states that have a REC program, a green energy

provider (such as a wind farm) is credited with one REC for every 1,000 kWh or 1 MWh of electricity it produces (for reference, an average residential customer consumes about 800 kWh in a month). A certifying agency gives each REC a unique identification number to make sure it doesn't get double-counted. The green energy is then fed into the electrical grid (by mandate), and the accompanying REC can then be sold on the open market.

Reference:
- U.S. EPA: http://www.epa.gov/greenpower/gpmarket/rec.htm

Retro-commissioning (RCx)
A systematic process that identifies operational and maintenance improvements in existing buildings with the objective of improving energy performance. RCx typically focuses on mechanical equipment, lighting and controls and usually optimizes existing system rather than replacing equipment. RCx typically includes an energy audit, diagnostic monitoring and functional tests. EPA offers guidance on retro-commissioning through its ENERGY STAR program.

Sustainable
The condition of being able to meet the needs of present generations without compromising resources for future generations.

Sustainable design and construction
A type of construction project that has resource conservation and occupant health and well-being as primary objectives of the design, engineering and construction processes.

Sustainable development
A pattern of resource use that aims to meet human needs while preserving the environment so that these needs can be met not only in the present, but also for future generations. Sustainable development, as a goal, aims to reconcile the carrying capacity of natural systems with the physical, social and cultural demands of the system's occupants. As defined by the Brundtland Commission in 1983, sustainable development is "development which meets the needs of the present without compromising the ability of future generations to meet their own needs."

Sustainable forest management
The management of forests according to the principles of sustainable development. This requires determining, in practical ways, how to use a forest today to ensure similar benefits, health and productivity in the future. Forest managers must assess and integrate a wide array of sometimes conflicting factors - commercial and non-commercial values, environmental considerations, community needs global impact - to produce sound forest plans. Voluntary sustainable forestry management guidance and certification is available through non-profits Forest Stewardship Council (FSC) and the Sustainable Forestry Initiative (SFI).

References:
- Forest Stewardship Council: http://www.fsc.org/
- Sustainable Forestry Initiative: http://www.sfiprogram.org/

Sustainable materials

Sustainable building materials are composed of renewable, rather than nonrenewable resources. Sustainable materials are environmentally responsible when their impacts are considered over the life of the product. Use of sustainable building materials can help reduce the environmental impacts associated with the extraction, transport, processing, fabrication, installation, reuse, recycling, and disposal of these source materials.

References:
- U.S. EPA: http://www.epa.gov/epp/
- NIBS: http://www.wbdg.org/resources/greenproducts.php
- National Institute of Standards and Testing (NIST): http://www.bfrl.nist.gov/oae/software/bees/

Sustainability Plan (SP)
A project-specific, written plan that enables the Construction Manager to coordinate efforts, track progress and focus energies on the deliverables and milestones required to satisfy project sustainability goals and requirements. A Sustainability Plan is both a guidance document and the foundation for a reporting system. It should be as concise as possible.

Transparency
A characteristic of non-opaque glass, transparency implies openness, dependable communication, and accountability. Transparent procedures include open meetings, financial disclosure statements, freedom of information rules, budgetary review, audits, etc. The concept of transparency is relevant to the practice of sustainable design and construction because measurement of outcomes relies upon generation of and access to meaningful, reliable data, and free exchange of qualitative information. Transparency is as much a culture value as it is a procedural framework.

U.S. Green Building Council (USGBC)
The U.S. Green Building Council is a non-profit organization devoted to shifting the building industry toward sustainability by providing information and standards on how buildings are designed, built and operated. The USGBC is best known for the development of the Leadership in Energy and Environmental Design (LEED®) rating system and Greenbuild, a green building conference.

Reference:
- U.S. Green Building Council: http://www.usgbc.org/

Volatile organic compounds
Organic chemical compounds with a high enough vapor pressure under normal conditions to enter the earth's atmosphere in large proportion. VOCs are numerous and varied. Although ubiquitous in nature and modern industrial society, they may also be harmful or toxic. VOCs, or subsets thereof, are often regulated. VOC are often the byproduct of curing or drying of industrial solvents and finishes, also known as "off-gassing."

Zero-energy building (ZEB)
A building with zero net energy consumption and zero carbon emissions annually. Zero-energy buildings can be used autonomously from the energy grid supply – energy can be harvested on-site. This definition does not include the emissions

generated in construction of the building and the embodied energy of its components. A ZEB generates the same amount of energy as is used, including the energy used to transport the energy to the building. (A building may be considered a ZEB if 100 percent of the energy it purchases comes from renewable energy sources, even if the energy is generated off the site.)

1.2.1 Project management

Sustainability, like cost, schedule, quality and safety, is a significant goal of project management.

Key responsibilities of the successful project manager with respect to sustainability include:

- Understanding the owner's requirements. A project with sustainability requirements may come with significant risk associated with new/emerging technologies or processes employed on the project. The project manager must clearly understand boundaries and expectations in order to practice a policy of "no surprises."

- Assist in the selection of appropriate designers and contractors. Projects with sustainability features will involve requirements that may be unique or new to designers, contractors and consultant. The project manager has a duty to assure that unique and distinctive project requirements are clearly identified and can thus be addressed or mitigated.

- Managing an inter-disciplinary project team. Project managers should be mindful that sustainable project requirements may add complexity through addition of team members, new/emerging features and technologies, and unfamiliar installation, testing or verification processes.

- Coordinating the activities of stakeholders. Sustainability requirements introduce complexity, stressing the importance of clear and consistent communication.

The project manager's primary tools to meet scope, schedule, budget and quality control objectives should be clearly articulated in the Project or Construction Management Plan and its component or subordinate elements. The following strategies for integrating sustainability requirements are suggested:

- The Sustainability Plan, which is unique to a project with sustainability goals and objectives, should clearly articulate project-specific sustainability goals, objectives and requirements, roles and responsibilities, and key mechanisms for coordinating efforts and tracking progress on the deliverables and milestones required to achieve goals and objectives and satisfy requirements. A Sustainability Plan is both a guidance document and the foundation for a reporting system. It should be as concise as possible.

- Commissioning Plan is based on the owner's project requirements, and requires significant input from the owner. The Commissioning Plan outlines training, sustainability certifications and requirements, installation and functional testing requirements, and operational requirements that will impact the owner after turnover.

- The Quality Management Plan (QMP) should include sustainability metrics. These metrics should be both thoroughly embedded in the Quality Management Plan by integrating performance, testing and inspection requirements for sustainability features, and separately identified as requisite elements of the project's sustainability program during construction so as to avert compromise by cost, schedule and scope control measures.

- Construction Procurement Plan should identify the contractual relationships and responsibilities of consultants and contractors charged with tasks related to delivering a project with sustainability requirements.

- Project Safety Plan: Projects with sustainability features or requirements may include installation of new or emerging technologies and equipment with which contractors, subcontractors, owners and CMs may have limited experience. Special care must be taken to clearly identify construction sequencing, testing and inspection processes in safe work plans.

- Contract administration procedures: While LEED or other sustainable design and construction requirements may be included in contract documents via reference, care should be taken to minimize coordination risks on the project's cost, schedule, scope and quality parameters by integrating sustainability requirements as much as possible in contract documents and project/program management procedures. Before inclusion or use on a project, standard documents should be reviewed and amended as required by legal counsel and insurance providers for project-specific application.

- The Project Procedures Manual should include procedures guiding the performance of tasks in design and construction that assure development and incorporation of the project's sustainability features.

- Management Information Systems: A project's Management Information System is the repository of project data and a project's computer-based "tool-set." Systems that may be considered part of a project's sustainability features include energy modeling and Building Information Modeling, which can facilitate high performance modeling, move the incorporation of sustainability features up in the design process, be used for LEED credit tracking, and support post-construction maintenance plans that optimize energy efficiency maintenance practices and capital replacement decisions. Project management procedures should clearly address update, input and output requirements and responsibilities and interface requirements. Provisions should be made for appropriate technical support and supervision.

Taken as a whole, the guidelines and tools of the project manager can be used to guide a project to successful implementation of sustainability requirements by a skilled and conscientious project manager and team.

References:
- CMAA Standards of Practice
- CMAA Project Management Guideline

1.2.2 Cost management

One of the CM's primary responsibilities is cost management and control. A successful CM achieves the goals of cost management and control by 1) developing a realistic, all-inclusive budget that meets the owner's goals, restrictions and limitations and 2) managing project risks in a manner that yields the best value project within the project budget. It is important to acknowledge the cost and risk profile of sustainability requirements and proactively apply cost management systems in a manner that protects and conserves the features they are designed to articulate.

The CM must work with the owner to establish sustainability goals and objectives, which will drive the design and engineering team's design development and preparation of contract documents. Sustainability expectations must be identified and clearly articulated as soon as possible in the project's life cycle, so that accurate budget estimates can be established, and the work scope is efficiently developed. Expectations, costs, and outcomes must be communicated to stakeholders as early as possible on a project with sustainability objectives that involves new or emerging technologies or processes so that appropriate talent is anticipated and secured – and associated cost risks are evaluated and contingencies established.

For instance, if a project is to be registered with the USGBC as a LEED certified project, the risk of achieving the prescribed level of certification may be managed by selecting an experienced design team to squire the engineering process, a commissioning consultant to manage commissioning and quality processes, and a LEED consultant specifically to manage LEED paperwork and submissions. The costs of specialty equipment and installation should be estimated early, and market forces that may impact the project identified and monitored with the objective of understanding alternative means to meet sustainability objectives within the project budget.

Sustainable projects may require early estimation and post-construction verification of project life cycle costs, or application of life cycle assessment (LCA) and alternatives analysis tools. The project team may include specialty consultants to conduct these studies. The CM should be well-versed in the principles and processes associated with these analyses.

The rapid development and evolution of emerging sustainability technologies may require that certain purchases of highly technical components be postponed so that the latest technology available is incorporated into the project. Adequate contingency for the owner, the designer and the contractors must be established to allow for potential cost increases for such items.

Standard cost management systems and fundamental project management best practices combined with an elevated vigilance of the cost risks related to new technologies and processes will help a project team meet sustainability goals and objectives within budget expectations.

References:
* CMAA Standards of Practice
* CMAA Cost Management Guideline

1.2.3 Time management

The CM is responsible for maintaining a focus on time management throughout the course of a project. The time implications of sustainable project features must be quantified - or carefully approximated. As with any other element of construction, the requirements and impacts of a project's sustainability features should be anticipated and monitored using standard scheduling tools so that the sustainability or high-performance features of a project are not knowingly sacrificed by failures in planning and management. Sustainable goals and objectives have to be built into the program for the project and not treated as an add-on feature if they are to be effective. This requires defining and including tasks associated with sustainable objectives in the Master Schedule, and assuring that other tools, such as Milestone Schedules, reflect activities required to meet sustainability goals.

Contract milestones addressing sustainable design and construction requirements should be considered and incorporated into contract documents.

In construction, time contingencies required for sustainable project elements must be built into the master and milestone schedules, and the CM must closely monitor the performance of subcontractors and suppliers responsible for these features. Inspection and verification practices integral to commissioning and quality management will help identify the need for intervention and mitigation.

Scheduling techniques range from relatively simple bar charts to critical path method (CPM) analysis and complex software programs. In general, scheduling software is an effective tool, but does not replace knowledge of basic planning and scheduling concepts and practices as means to achieve sustainability goals.

For a project with sustainability features that rely on new technologies, practices or means and methods, the CM's should thoroughly understand new technology and applications, performance and installations requirements, staging, phasing considerations and quality processes. Nothing can replace a vigilant CM that is thoroughly aware of the manner in which a project's execution delivers on the promise of its design principles, including sustainability.

References:
- CMAA Standards of Practice
- CMAA Time Management Guideline

1.2.4 Quality management

"Quality" is the degree to which the project and its components meet the owner's expectations, objectives, standards, and intended purpose. Quality is determined by measuring conformity of the project to the plans, specifications and applicable standards. When an owner decides to include the principles of sustainability in a project's expectations and objectives, this intent must be borne out by design solutions, and its requirements embedded in implementation plans and metrics of project success.

Quality management is the process of planning, organizing, implementing, monitoring and documenting a system of policies and procedures that assign, coordinate and direct relevant project resources and activities in a manner that will achieve project objectives and performance requirements. A project with sustainability features systematically applies its quality management system to yield healthful, durable, and environmentally or ecologically sound performance throughout the facility life cycle – from pre-design, planning, construction, post-construction and into the operation and maintenance stage.

Embedding sustainability in the quality management system involves transforming sustainability goals and requirements into critical project metrics and milestones using traditional quality management and control methodologies. The Quality Management Plan and related procedures and documentation is made to clearly articulate the goals, plans, performance indicators and verification processes necessary to demonstrate the achievement of sustainability objectives. The quality management system is adjusted to:

- Include sustainability reviews;
- Identify sustainability-specific elements of traditional reviews;
- Identify metrics that capture intermediate and ultimate performance parameters;
- Include sustainability-specific hold-points, milestones and performance objectives in checklists, record-keeping and document control systems, often as the Commissioning Plan and procedures; and
- Leverage commissioning: Specify testing and verification processes to assure compliance and enable continuous improvement.

If a project requires attainment of a specific sustainable building system rating, such as LEED, Green Globes or Energy Star, procedures are adapted or devised to monitor the responsibilities and obligations of each project participant involved in the process, including submission and processing of relevant certification documentation, requests for information reasonably necessary to obtain an appropriate written certification, and notification by the designating body or organization that the intended certification level or status is achieved.

16

The Commissioning Agent or Green Building Facilitator should be a party to the quality management organization, and the input of the Commissioning Agent and/or Green Building Facilitator should be sought and incorporated in quality and project management document and procedures.

The CM must be knowledgeable of the performance requirements; applicable green building rating system, if any; and the means, methods and limitations of sustainability measures. The CM's responsibilities may include:

- Assist in setting sustainability goals;
- Advise on budget implications of sustainability measures;
- Advise on schedule implications of sustainability measures;
- Advise on public acceptance matters;
- Assist with design consultant, sustainability consultant (or "green building facilitator") and contractor selection;
- Assist in evaluating alternatives to achieve sustainability goals;
- Assist in providing verification of progress and achievement of sustainability objectives; and
- Assist in sustainability impact analyses, value engineering and other studies to assure or verify the achievement of sustainability goals.

References:
- CMAA Standards of Practice
- CMAA Quality Management Guideline

1.2.5 Contract administration

Contract administration is the function of implementing the terms and conditions of a contract, based upon established systems, policies, and procedures. The key contract administration tools are the Project or Construction Management Plan, the Sustainability Plan and the Project Procedures Manual. The Construction Management Plan outlines the project scope, the milestone schedule, the budget, the team organization, the strategy to be used in contracting and procurement, and the basic systems to be utilized. The Project Procedures Manual details the specific processes intended to yield key performance objectives - cost, schedule, scope and quality.

When a project includes sustainability goals or features, contract administration efforts must include the means to ascertain compliance with sustainability objectives, and control the outcome to yield a project that complies with contract documents. The CM should develop or cause the development of submittal procedures early in the project – in the pre-design phase if possible – to provide for recording and controlling the flow of submittals required by the GBF.

References:
- CMAA Standards of Practice
- CMAA Contract Administration Guideline

1.2.6 Professional practice

While the concept of sustainable, green or high-performance design and construction are considered mainstream, the regulatory environment governing sustainable projects varies among local and state governments, public and private sector decision-makers and funding parties. Furthermore, the sustainability lexicon can vary depending on project type, performance expectations and regulatory jurisdiction. CMs should research applicable local and state codes and standards for guidance.

The real and perceived importance of sustainable development, design and construction practices nevertheless grows, driven by advances in climate and biodiversity science, and a growing consensus that responsible development requires the construction industry to embrace practices that are sensitive to ecological and environmental factors.

Government units with significant interest and influence in sustainability factors include:

- U.S. Environmental Protection Agency (EPA);
- U.S. Department of Energy (DOE);
- U.S. Department of Defense (DOD); and
- U.S. Department of the Interior (DOI).

Applicable federal standards codes and standards include:

- ASTM E2432—Standard Guide for the General Principles of Sustainability Relative to Building;
- Energy Independence and Security Act (EISA 2007);
- Energy Policy Act of 2005; and
- Executive Order 13423, "Strengthening Federal Environmental, Energy, and Transportation Management."

Materials performance and energy efficiency of systems, equipment and building components and assemblies is typically addressed in the governing building code by reference to national standards and consensus standards developed by non-governmental organizations (NGOs) comprising professional societies, government-sponsored research and development organizations, universities and private sector companies. Most professional societies offer discipline and sector-specific information and training in sustainable, green or high performance practices. In addition to CMAA, these include:

- ASHRAE: American Society of Heating, Refrigeration and Air-Conditioning Engineers;
- ASME: American Society of Mechanical Engineers;
- ASCE: American Society of Civil Engineers;
- ANSI: American National Standards Institute;
- ASTM: American Society of Testing and Measurement;
- IEEE: Institute of Electrical and Electronics Engineers; and
- UL: Underwriters Laboratories.

Knowledge of the sustainability domain is essential for a CM. CMAA strongly encourages professionals to leverage the resources most closely aligned with their professional training and work assignments, and to take advantage of professional development opportunities offered by professional societies, regulatory agencies and certification authorities.

Finally, consensus guidelines for the building industry have been developed by organizations dedicated to bringing the principles and goals of sustainability to market. These include:

- U.S. Green Building Council (USGBC), which developed and maintains the Leadership in Energy and Environmental Design (LEED) rating system, and the LEED Accredited Professional credential; and
- Green Building Institute (GBI), which developed and maintains the Green Globes guidance and assessment program, and the Green Globes Professional Certification.

Reference:
- CMAA Standards of Practice

1.2.7 Safety

Safety management involves anticipating and implementing procedures to protect the health and safety of all people on a project site: workers, visitors, and the general public. Safety management is a risk management strategy for loss control that is designed to protect against the cost of damage, injury, treatment and remediation of life and property. As such, standard safety provisions on a construction project include minimum safety education and training, and insurance.

A safe job is consistent with sustainable practices. Safety applies to the safety of workers and the public due to the way a job is run during construction. In the case of many projects with sustainability features safety also applies to the features that confer a healthy working environment after construction is complete due, for instance, to protected and cleaned ductwork, low VOCs, properly functioning air handling, heating and cooling systems, and low GHG emissions.

A measure of safety is the Experience Modification Rate (EMR) which is a multiplier used by the insurance industry to gauge past cost of injuries, risk of future injuries, and determine the cost of workers' compensation during construction. An EMR of 1.0 is considered average; an EMR less than 1.0 is good; an EMR of greater than 1.0 is relatively poor, which will be reflected in a higher relative construction bid because an insurer's workers compensation rates will be elevated. Another measure of safety performance is Occupational Safety and Health (OSHA) incident rate for "recordable injuries" and "lost time Injuries," and OSHA publishes average industry results for these rates annually for various types and markets of construction.

For projects with sustainability features that involve new or emerging technologies and contractors with relatively little experience, EMRs and incident rates may be relatively high as a result of meager data. Special care should be given to all work elements and areas involving new or emerging technologies or processes, with particular vigilance to the development and deployment of safe work plans that describe the work sequence, hold-points, inspections, hazards, means and methods.

As "communicator-in-chief," the project manager is responsible for assuring that the importance of safety and the mechanisms to preserve life and property are communicated to project participants.

Reference:
• CMAA Standards of Practice

1.2.8 Risk management

In the context of design and construction, risk management is the methodical application of management processes designed to reduce the negative impact of uncertainties on a project's cost, schedule and quality expectations. The potential consequences of risk include financial losses, damages and other undesirable events – including the loss of opportunities. Risk, inherent on major capital construction projects, may be heightened on a project with sustainability objectives due to a range of uncertainties, including:

• Unproven contractor performance on a project with LEED requirements;
• Unproven performance of new or emerging technologies;
• Unproven consultant, contractor, subcontractor or supplier performance for new or emerging technologies;
• Uncertain impact of commodities pricing affecting sustainability features of a project, e.g., components of photovoltaic equipment, volatile commodities (energy) pricing;
• Lack of experienced technical or specialty subcontractors;
• Delay in finalizing certain details association with emerging technologies and equipment in order to assure that the "latest" technology possible is employed in the project, thereby potentially impacting final pricing or the project schedule;
• Unrealistic owner expectations;
• Potential contract issues in which contract compliance is controlled by a third party. e.g. Certification to a LEED standard may be a contract requirement and the scoring to achieve a certain LEED level is somewhat subjectively determined by a third party rather than performance based and can be complicated by owner driven changes; and
• Inadequate budget allocation or increased cost for sustainability related materials and systems.

Risk is most effectively managed by reducing uncertainties. The impact of uncertainties that cannot be eliminated must be managed using contingencies to establish boundary expectations. Risk can be eliminated or reduced through investigation, design and engineering that reduces uncertainty, or through various means of transfer to another party, including use of insurance products.

Risk management efforts should be evaluated at meetings throughout each project phase. To assure adequate vigilance to sustainability objectives, sustainability-specific status and challenges should be discussed as a separate agenda item.

Reference:
* CMAA Standards of Practice

1.2.9 Building Information Modeling (BIM)

BIM is a process by which digital representations of the physical and functional characteristics of a facility are captured, analyzed, documented, and assessed virtually, then revised iteratively through the design and construction process. BIM enables 3D parametric modeling, engineering analysis, clash detection, 4D schedules, quantity take-off, and general information assignment (including specification and product data linkage).

BIM has the potential to reduce the cost of sustainable design by making design and engineering information routinely available as standard byproduct of the design process.

BIM offers a collaboration and project delivery platform that meets the needs of project participants across the project life cycle, including those responsible for assessing whether the project will meet the criteria of credit-driven sustainability programs like LEED. Because BIM can incorporate accurate modeling information early in the design process, BIM can improve coordination and reduce potential errors associated with assessing sustainability performance. As-built conditions can be incorporated into a project's BIM to help determine if it is being built within specified design tolerances and will achieve specified credits.

BIM can be used to model facility orientation, window placement and lighting long before a project is built, and is thus well-suited to assess daylight modeling and solar access, both of which can factor into a project's LEED credit profile. Furthermore, BIM can play a powerful role on a project with sustainability goals because it moves design decisions into the hands of designers by producing calculations involving lighting, site analysis, energy use and water use in support of trade-off considerations and design decisions.

BIM can be used throughout construction to analyze and communicate the building process in a virtual environment, including sequence of work, means and methods, logistics and documentation of as-built conditions. BIM can provide the project team with ongoing analyses such as:

* How much recycled content is being incorporated – for individual components and for the entire facility; and
* The quantity of construction material that is sourced within a certain radius.

BIM's utility continues throughout the life of the facility, with the model serving as a shared knowledge resource for information about a facility. The model serves as a reliable basis for decisions throughout a facility's life cycle – from inception through design to construction, occupancy and operation.

The CM wishing to leverage BIM on a project with sustainability features must take care to select a system that represents the facility as an integrated database of coordinated information that meets the team's expectations for modeling and management of the design and construction process, including functions that will facilitate the sustainability program.

References:
* CMAA Standards of Practice
* NIBS Facilities Information Council National BIM Standard: http://www.wbdg.org/bim/nibs_bim.php

2.0 Pre-Design Phase

2.1 Introduction

The pre-design phase may be the first opportunity for the CM to apply the construction management process toward meeting the objectives of a sustainable project. The pre-design phase is the period before schematic design commences during which the project is initiated and the program is developed; the planning and conceptual stage.

2.1.1 Sustainability Plan: establish owner sustainability goals, objectives and requirements

The CM's first priority is to understand the owner's sustainability goals and objectives.

Many conceptual design and estimating iterations may be required before a project meets the owner's time, cost, quality, sustainability and other and performance requirements. Once these requirements are established and approved by the owner, the team must be committed to completing the project within those requirements.

Sustainability goals, objectives and requirements can range from low to high impact and anything in between:

- Seeking a specified rating in accordance with design guidelines such as LEED, Green Globes or Energy Star;
- Specification of whole-building commissioning;
- Achievement of energy or water efficiency performance at some verifiable level above code;
- Commitment to off-grid or net-zero energy performance;
- Adoption of a "paperless office" management system;
- Use of Building Information Modeling (BIM) to optimize efficiency in design, construction and facility operation;
- Commitment to use materials and products from an environmentally preferred purchasing database endorsed by a trusted "green" product certification program such as U.S. EPA, Green Seal, EcoLogo, Scientific Certification Systems, MBDC Cradle to Cradle;
- Inclusion of performance monitoring and verification systems; and
- Commitment to local workforce employment or development goals (and other environmental justice goals).

Sustainability goals, objectives and requirements are the basis of critical follow-on activities:

- Development of the Sustainability Plan:
  - Part of the Project and Construction Management Plan(s);
  - Multi-disciplinary effort for team-building and communication;
  - Objectives include articulation of goals and desired outcomes, identification of impacts and mitigation strategies, and establishment of monitoring and control mechanisms appropriate to the sustainability program;
  - Determine how sustainability requirements will be integrated into the Quality Management System; and
  - Begin outlining processes and procedures for inclusion in procedures manuals.
- Team development:
  - Include a party responsible for coordinating the cooperation and performance of project participants towards the fulfillment of sustainability goals and objectives; and
  - Specialty sub consultants or subcontractors needed to facilitate achievement of sustainability goals and objectives.
- Staff development;
- Develop plans and procedures;
- Establish project budget and appropriate levels of contingency;
- Establish master schedules and work sequences; and
- Procurement planning.

For instance, if "paperless office" is a project goal, subsequent activities include:

- Selection of online program management service provider;
- Staffing decisions required to meet technical support needs;
- Assuring that project management plans and procedures provide guidance to all project participants on work-flow and document control requirements, with the objective of assuring efficient, effective work-flow and timely decision-making in a paperless environment;
- Including team-wide costs of paperless office costs in the budget; considerations of efficiencies or disadvantages on productivity;
- Identifying paperless capability milestones for project participants; include training completion milestones;
- Identifying equipment, training and use requirements in consultant and construction contract documents; and
- Consulting with legal counsel to determine applicable limitations associated with recent or pending court decisions required to properly protect all parties.

In short, project goals and objectives should be articulated clearly and unambiguously in documents that will inform subsequent decisions and management systems throughout the course of the project, and be used to measure the project team's success.

2.1.2 Scope of services

Contract documents for consultants, subconsultants, contractors and subcontractors should be modified to reflect:

- Sustainability goals, objectives and requirements;
- Contract requirements for a sustainability "rating" or certification (LEED, Green Globes, etc), if applicable;
- Project sustainability performance requirements, if applicable;
- Project sustainability features or measures, as applicable;
- Project sustainability features or measures that require specific verification or documentation; and
- Documentation required to verify completion of tasks or fulfillment of measures associated with sustainability goals and objectives.

Sustainability goals, objectives and requirements must be incorporated into a document that describes the sustainability program approach and "preliminary sustainability scorecard." Programming by the architect should include both documents, and time should be allotted for developing both of these deliverables and to evaluate them as they will influence process and budget.

Specific guidelines and codes should be referenced and included in contract documents. Consider using ConsensusDOCSTM 310 Green Building Addendum, which includes guidance and provisions for identifying project expectations and participant roles and responsibilities, instituting procedures, and addressing risk allocation on projects with sustainability requirements.

2.1.3 Selection of a design team

The owner must assemble a team of design and construction management professionals that will define and develop the project and organize the activities of project participants.

Depending on the type and complexity of the project and its sustainability features, the owner should be encouraged to consider design consultants with experience and distinct responsibilities for the sustainable design and construction program, such as:

- A/E with sustainable design and construction experience, and technical subconsultants with requisite experience, including BIM experience, if required.

- Commissioning Agent (CA), responsible for planning and overseeing the Building Commissioning Process and specific commissioning activities. The criteria for a good CA is a balance of lead engineering design experience with extensive field experience in installing and testing mechanical and electrical equipment and systems. Common approaches to structuring commissioning roles and responsibilities include:

    - Independent Agent as CA—the most common approach;

- CM as CA—An effective and economical approach when the CM is independent of the contractor's team (not "at-risk") and has the requisite technical experience; and
- A/E as CA (not typical).

Owners should consider requiring the CA to possess a recognized certification or credential (see 2.1.4).

- Sustainable design consultant or "Green Building Facilitator" to coordinate the collaboration of project participants with respect to sustainability project deliverables and goals, record-keeping and verification processes. This may be the CA, party to the project team, or a separate contractor.

Consultants should be selected based on general suitability and verifiable past performance on work of a similar nature.

Responsibilities and requirements for the sustainability reviews should be clearly articulated in A/E, CM, CA and GBF contracts.

2.1.4 Commissioning Agent (CA) qualifications

A CA has technical background and depth of expertise with the commissioning process including verification techniques, functional performance testing, system equipment and operations and maintenance (O&M) knowledge. The CA should have significant in-building commissioning experience, including technical and management expertise on projects of similar scope, size and type. The CA should bring a total building commissioning perspective to the project, be knowledgeable in national building fire codes, detection systems, LEED, energy efficiency imperatives and demonstrate experience with Federal requirements. CA certifications are offered by the Building Commissioning Association and others.

References:
- ASHRAE: http://www.ashrae.org/certification/page/2086
- Building Commissioning Association: http://www.bcxa.org/certification/index.htm

2.1.5 Sustainable design guidance

Many states and municipalities have developed design guidelines with regional and local relevance. Separate agencies in larger municipalities may have different green design requirements. School districts tend to have developed guidance.

Federal government agencies have adopted high performance facility requirements. GSA requires that all new construction projects and substantial renovations must achieve a LEED Silver certification, although GSA encourages project teams to exceed LEED® Silver and achieve LEED® Gold.

Cursory research will yield an abundance of guidance on application of sustainable design principles for various facility types.

References:
- ASTM E2432 – Standard Guide for the General Principles of Sustainability Relative to Buildings: http://www.astm.org/Standards/E2432.htm
- ASHRAE: http://www.ashrae.org/
- U.S. GBC LEED: http://www.usgbc.org/

2.1.6 Project delivery strategies

The owner, owner's legal counsel must adopt a suitable governing contract strategy to deliver sustainable design and construction goals. Irrespective of the contracting method, the owner and owner's counsel must establish risk allocation strategies in contract documents. Contracts should:

- Identify responsibility for the achievement of sustainability measures;
- Articulate liability provisions;
- Characterize damages as consequential in order to be addressed more fully in underlying governing contracts; and
- Define and provide for damages that could reasonably be incurred by the owner as a consequence of the project not achieving specified sustainability features.

CM-at-Risk
CM-at-Risk is a delivery method in which the CM is contracted to deliver the project within the owner's budget, in many cases pursuant to a Guaranteed Maximum Price (GMP). On a CM-at-Risk project, the CM acts on the owner's behalf to facilitate and coordinate design, and continues as the equivalent of a general contractor during the construction phase. To mitigate the CM's exposure to risks on a CM-at-Risk project with sustainability features, a CM must have a thorough understanding of associated cost, schedule and quality considerations.

Design-build
Design-build (or design/build) is a project delivery system characterized by the owner conveying contractual responsibility for design development, engineering and construction to a single entity, thereby enabling overlap of the design and construction phase, and encouraging collaboration between the builder and the engineer. This system is promoted as a means to mitigate project risk and reduce the delivery schedule. Design-build can contribute achieving project sustainability features by bringing the builder's practical experience to bear on the planning and design of sustainability elements at an early stage.

Integrated Project Delivery (IPD)
Integrated Project Delivery is a relatively new approach that seeks to align goals and improve collaboration. The approach can contribute to the probability of successful sustainability features by bringing the builder's practical experience to bear on the planning and design of sustainability elements at an early stage. Few projects incorporate all of the common IPD characteristics, and other project delivery projects

can use some or all of the characteristics. There are many variations but most IPD projects have some of the following characteristics.

- A multi-party contract signed by the owner and an architect (or A/E) and a CM (or general contractor) instead of separate contractors with each. Other key consultants or subcontractors may be added.

- A management committee, with representative from the core team participants, including the owner.

- Shared risks and incentives for core team members based on jointly developed goals.

- Transparent processes and open-book financials.

- An emphasis on collaborative decision-making.

- Approaches to reduce litigation such as waivers or dispute resolution ladders.

- Significant collaboration by the builder(s) in design.

- Lean construction principles.

- The use of collaboration software such a BIM and PMIS.

- Co-location of project teams and open communication.

Design-bid-build
A traditional approach that involves design and production of contract documents by an architect/engineer (A/E), followed by competitively bidding the project to a third party contractor. Risks to realizing the sustainability features of a project can be mitigated through clear and complete contract and bid documents that anticipate and mitigate threats to sustainability features.

Energy performance contracting
A procurement process that is emerging as a preferred method for some energy efficiency improvement projects, which allows clients to use future energy cost savings to pay for new energy-efficient equipment and services. A number of states use energy performance contracts to reduce energy consumption in state-owned buildings, typically by 15 percent to 35 percent in selected facilities. Energy performance contracts typically provide for a guarantee that cost savings will meet or exceed payments for equipment and services over the contract period. Owners assemble an in-house team, often with the assistance of a third party energy consultant, and conduct a preliminary assessment to determine the facilities with the greatest potential for energy savings. Once the preliminary assessment is complete, the owner identifies an energy service company (ESCO) with

experience, and selects an ESCO through competitive bidding and qualification processes. Once an ESCO is selected, the owner conducts an investment-grade energy audit to identify potential energy cost saving measures. When approved, the audit results can be used to develop a comprehensive plan of action. The ESCO proposes this plan, including the anticipated costs, to the agency. This plan forms the basis for performance contract, or PC. Owners can negotiate with ESCOs so that the PC clearly defines the length of the contract, the roles and responsibilities of each party, maintenance expectations, staff training, the method for measuring and verifying savings, a savings guarantee, financing terms, etc. A clearly defined protocol for determining energy cost savings is essential to an effective PC. All parties must understand how energy cost savings will be measured and verified, especially if savings are to be shared.

2.1.7 Project implementation tools

The CM typically uses several management tools to communicate a project's requirements to all stakeholders and advance the project in an organized manner. Each of these tools should be modified to clearly identify sustainability goals and objectives, sustainable project features and measures, and roles/responsibilities for same.

Project Management Plan
The CM should assure that the Project or Construction Management Plan clearly identifies:

- Project sustainability goals, objectives, requirements, reporting requirements and milestones;
- Roles and responsibilities for coordination of sustainability activities designed to yield sustainability features, deliverables, record-keeping, verification measures, etc.; and
- Risk management strategies.

Sustainability Plan
A project-specific, plan that enables the CM to coordinate efforts, track progress and focus energies on the deliverables and milestones required to satisfy project sustainability goals and requirements. A Sustainability Plan is both a guidance document and the foundation for a reporting system. It should be as concise as possible and identify:

- Project sustainability goals, objectives, requirements:
  - Include a preliminary sustainability checklist or scorecard;
- Roles and responsibilities for coordination of sustainability activities designed to yield sustainability features, deliverables, record-keeping, verification measures, etc.;
- Sustainability reporting requirements and milestones; and
- Risk management strategies.

Because the requirements of sustainability on a project must be integrated into all other management documents and contract documents, the Sustainability Plan should be among the first documents produced by the project team. It should be succinct.

Project Commissioning Plan
In the pre-design phase, the owner's requirements are documented and established as the foundation for design, construction and occupancy in the form of the Commissioning Plan.

The Commissioning Plan outlines the organization, schedule, allocation of resources, and documentation requirements of the commissioning process, which is a quality focused process for enhancing the delivery of a project. The process focuses upon verifying and documenting that the facility and all of its systems and assemblies are planned, designed, installed, tested, operated, and maintained to meet the owner's project requirements.

The Commissioning Plan establishes the framework for managing and handling commissioning. A preliminary Commissioning Plan is essential to all commissioned projects provides the structure for all project participants to anticipate and plan for commissioning requirements and milestones. The plan is first developed during the pre-design phase and is updated at or near design completion. During the pre-design phase, the Commissioning Plan focuses on incorporating the owner's performance requirements and integrating them into the construction documents. (Details of systems tests and procedures, assembly specific checklists, and testing and documentation responsibilities are incorporated in Construction Phase Commissioning Plans.) Commissioning Plans typically include the following sections or content:

- General Project Information;
- Overview and Scope of the Project Commissioning;
- Commissioning Protocols and Communications;
- Commissioning Process, including Team Responsibilities;
- Commissioning Schedule;
- Commissioning Documentation; and
- Appendices:
    - Testing and Inspection Plans;
    - Change Management Procedures;
    - Pre-Functional and Functional Test Procedures;
    - Construction Checklists; and
    - Issues Logs.

All project stakeholders should participate in this process and become familiar with the program. With each subsequent phase, it is the duty of the CA to verify that the program is being met, or through change management procedures document how the program/scope has changed and again seek sign-off from all stakeholders.

(For a project to be LEED certified, commissioning process activities must comply with the prerequisite requirements for fundamental building commissioning requirements.)

Reference:
- ASHRAE Guideline-0-2005, "The Commissioning Process": http://www.ashrae.org/publications/page/1279

Project procedures

The Project Procedures Manual must include procedures related to sustainability, and sustainability-specific issues must in turn be reflected in all other project procedures for all phases of the project.

Project procedures on a project with sustainability typically address:

- Sustainability review;
- Configuration or change management;
- Commissioning requirements in all phases;
- C&D waste management requirements
- Air quality controls;
- Sustainable project document control; and
- BIM procedures, all phases, all parties.

Building Information Modeling (BIM)

Building Information Modeling (BIM) is the process of generating and managing building data during its life cycle that leverages three-dimensional, real-time, dynamic building modeling software to increase productivity in building design and construction. BIM is enabled by modeling software that incorporates building geometry, spatial relationships, geographic information, and the quantities and properties of building components. Utilizing BIM has the potential to save project time and cost on a sustainable project because calculations and trade-off analyses are enabled earlier in the process, facilitating earlier design decisions and improving collaboration and coordination.

The same features can minimize rework and construction errors: BIM's single data entry into one model helps manage inconsistency and error due to manual and multiple input. Once entered or altered, data becomes available in the single current model to all project participants. BIM can be used to "rehearse" construction processes, including project sustainability features, and help identify conflicts and their resolution before actual construction dollars are spent.

Finally, BIM can generate the data needed for project sustainability certification(s).

A decision as to the extent and process of BIM use is critical as soon as possible is the project so that procedures for BIM use may be communicated to all parties.

Management Information System (MIS)
The system should enable secure and the efficient capture and output of project data required for reporting and forecasting, and should meet the data management and reporting requirements of a project with sustainability goals and objectives that may require discrete reporting.

The reliability and accuracy of data capture, storage and reporting functions of the MIS are critical on projects implemented by ESCOs or other parties with carbon footprint or GHG reduction targets that are integral to financing mechanisms.

Project personnel with knowledge of sustainability and commissioning reporting requirements should be consulted as early as possible on formats, data management requirements, distribution and frequency of reports, and policies for records retention.

If Building Information Modeling (BIM) is to be used on the project, BIM development, modification and management procedures should be clearly articulated in a separate document and incorporated in all other project management procedures. BIM interface with data management and reporting systems should be anticipated.

Reference:
- NIBS Facilities Information Council National BIM Standard

Pre-design project conference
The CM should plan, conduct and document a pre-design project conference, the objective of which is to establish a clear understanding in all project participants of the roles, responsibilities goals and process requirements, as articulated in the project and other management plans and procedures. Sustainability goals and objectives should be clearly articulated as a mission-critical aspect of the project. Risks and risk mitigation strategies for project sustainability should be conveyed to participants. The pre-design conference agenda should explicitly include:

- Project description and scope definition;
- Project cost, schedule, quality and sustainability targets;
- Control;
- Decision-making authorities;
- Roles and responsibilities of project participants;
- Management reporting and roles; and
- Meeting frequencies and deliverables.

3.0 Design Phase

3.1 Introduction

The goal of design is to turn the owner's desires and the design team's proposed solutions into a detailed set of specifications and drawings. The outcome of the design phase is a set of documents that describes the project in terms of all requisite parameters, which can be issued for construction or for bid to a third-party contracting community. Sustainability goals and objectives are thoroughly subsumed in the design process, and specified as any other program requirement by way of drawings, details, instructions to the contractor, specifications and references.

As design proceeds from schematic through final design, the team must repeatedly consider life cycle costs vs. benefit with respect to the desired or mandated sustainability goals or requirements. The earlier in the design process that a decision regarding the acceptable first costs of sustainability features can be made, the more cost effective the design process will be. First costs of sustainability and life cycle benefits are optimized through periodic trade-off analyses, life cycle and sustainability reviews, value engineering and alternatives analysis and energy performance modeling.

3.1.1 "Design to principle"

Many advocates and practitioners of sustainable development and design acknowledge that not all impacts can be monetized and thus readily considered in traditional cost-benefit analysis. These are known as "negative externalities." The atmosphere is considered a "global commons" into which individuals and firms release GHG, compensation for which cannot easily be secured through usage fees or taxes. The consequences of unregulated emissions are borne by all irrespective of their contribution to GHG levels.

Few controls exist for carbon dioxide (CO_2), the major greenhouse gas, which has no short-term damaging effects at ground level. Atmospheric accumulations of carbon dioxide and other GHGs will have significant effects on global climates and climate cycles, with great uncertainty as to impact, probable scale, onset and attenuation.

An owner that specifies sustainability features on a project either responds to a government mandate that effectively eliminates cost-consciousness of sustainability features through regulation, or signals a willingness to assume some cost risk greater than can be reasonably expected to benefit the corporate bottom line and the traditional return on investment calculation.

The monetary value of negative externalities and their preponderance on projects with sustainability objectives in today's markets requires that project participants take care to look beyond traditional cost-benefit equations to assure that broader sustainability goals are met in accordance with principles and not traditional return on investment calculations.

3.1.2 Design management and administration

The various phases of design should be defined by the A/E contract. During each of the following phases, the A/E is responsible for developing deliverables and documents that reflect the work product of their professional service:

- Conceptual;
- Schematic;
- Design Development;
- Construction Documents; and
- Support during Construction.

The project team should take specific care to review the status of sustainability goals, objectives and requirements along with all other project parameters (cost, schedule, quality).

Those parties not directly involved in design development but having a potential significant contribution to project sustainability goals should be made aware of all progress on the project and requested to furnish their input. This is especially important as the project nears the 90 percent phase and the bid phase. Any input from the CA, operation and maintenance forces, facility users, and others may need to be coordinated by the design team prior to the issuance of bid documents. In some situations, the CM and, possibly, the owner may request that certain associated parties to the contract actually sign-off on progress documents and the final submission of the design to limit any chance that full coordination has not been accomplished. Involvement of the party designated as the GBF is essential.

The CM should include sustainability in the detailed checklists that confirm or verify the achievement of design goals in plans, specifications, and estimates at each stage of design completion.

Owner authorization and approvals
Procedures to secure the authorization and approval of the owner to maintain progress and proceed with the project must consider sustainability. This is a non-trivial matter, as tension may exist between sustainability goals and cost and schedule parameters or other performance objectives. Explicit review of the impact of scope schedule or budget changes or adjustments on sustainability objectives - and vice versa - should be clearly identified, and triggers established to bring any conflict to the appropriate authority for resolution.

Quality Management System (QMS)

Quality control is achieved through a system of detailed checks and reviews between members of the design team. These are used to verify the performance of requisite activities such as confirmation of viability of the design and design assumptions, check of calculations, and coordination across disciplines. The quality control system should include measures for verification and validation of tasks that protect and maintain a project's sustainability requirements. Quality Assurance activities confirm that quality control activities are carried out that protect and maintain the integrity of a project's sustainability requirements.

Changes in design scope or criteria
The design of the project is an evolutionary process. During the course of the project, change is inevitable. The CM must monitor the changes and advise the owner of any associated cost and time impacts. Notification by the designer together with the review of the progress documents will identify variances with the previously agreed-upon design criteria. The variances can have a positive or negative cost or schedule impact on the project. The status of project sustainability performance and commitments must be evaluated as part of the variance review process.

The cost of the project must be carefully tracked and monitored for every change. When sustainability is an explicit element of the project, the CM should first assure that appropriate requirements are included in the design documents, and subsequently, that impacts of changes on sustainable project features are duly identified and mitigated. Vigilance is particularly critical to identify the impact of a change on a project's LEED credit profile, Green Globes score, or the integrity of any other sustainable design rating system.

When sustainability objectives are jeopardized by a change in scope or design criteria, the design team must be alerted and allowed sufficient time to mitigate or otherwise adjust in response to the owner's priorities for the project.

All design criteria changes and their impacts must be communicated to the project team. The efficiency of the team can be affected by these changes.

Document control
The CM is the clearinghouse for all project communications. The Document Control and MIS systems should be devised, from the beginning, to identify elements critical to the project's sustainability program. This is particularly critical on a project with LEED or other green building rating system documentation requirements.

Contract documents
Contract documents should clearly define the elements of the work designed to yield sustainability features of the project. Ideally, specific sustainability parameters should be written into the contract

documents. Required documentation, monitoring, independent agents, and other requirements should all be clearly defined and written into the contract documents.

Standard formatting from the Construction Specifications Institute (CSI) is used throughout the construction industry to format construction specifications in building contracts. The format facilitates location of specific types of information. CSI's MasterFormat2004™ is organized in 50 divisions, each of which contains a number of sections. Sections are divided into three parts—"general," "products," and "execution." Each part is organized by a standardized system of articles and paragraphs. Green building specifications can be easily incorporated into CSI MasterFormat2004™ by:

- Adding a section on Environmental Protection Procedures to Division 1 that states the project's environmental goals, and including other environmental specifications, such as general requirements for recycled content levels and a Construction and Demolition (C&D) Waste Management Plan. This section can also include a statement that requires contractors to establish a C&D Waste Management Plan at the pre-construction conference.

- Including technical specifications in Divisions 2 through 50 providing for high performance building materials, including material types and installation methods.

- Including language that specifies that work is performed in a manner consistent with the environmental goals of the project. The incorporation of a green material alone may not contribute to "greening" the project if it does not function as intended due to improper installation or if it becomes contaminated as the result of careless handling.

- Explicitly articulating contractual "sustainability" requirements, and differentiating these from sustainability "goals."

If verification and documentation activities are required to achieve a specified sustainable facility rating, this should be clearly identified in contract documents. For instance, intent for a project to be LEED certified with the USGBC should be formally noted as such within the bid documents. If the owner and designer choose NOT to have the project formally registered with the USGBC but intend for it to be a LEED equivalent project this too must be defined within the bid documents. BIM requirements should also be clearly identified.

Permits
The CM should assure that a list of project required permits for the project is developed. The list must include applicable Federal, State and Local permits and indicate the responsibility for obtaining the permit. The list should include submittal schedule for LEED, Green

Globes or another sustainable design or rating system, where applicable.

3.1.3 Design review

The CM should periodically review the design documents, focusing on the need for clarity, consistency and coordination among the Contractor(s). Pursuant to the CM's contract, the CM should participate in a sustainability review of the documents to review that sustainability goals, objectives and requirements are being addressed, evaluate the reasonableness of constraints placed on the contractor, and verify that the documents are sufficiently clear on these points.

Sustainability reviews
The sustainability checklist or scorecard should be reviewed and updated as documents progress to reflect specific measures and features of the project. The checklist should be reviewed following every design review and prior to sign-off of every design phase to verify inclusion of sustainability measures, or compliance with sustainability requirements. This process in itself generally has little effect on the schedule, but the result of this review and update may be cause for the team to revisit objectives and approaches to the sustainable program which may impact the schedule.

The CM should periodically determine if relevant and appropriate criteria are well defined in the construction documents. When the project is expected to meet specific sustainability thresholds or rating levels, the CM should also verify that the construction documents accurately identify the certification and necessary documentation, and indicate the party or parties responsible for associated activities. The A/E contract should specify periodic sustainability reviews during design throughout design so that sustainability objectives and requirements are incorporated.

Constructability review
The CM is often required to review design documents for constructability, or reasonableness and efficiency in construction with the objective of maximizing the ease and efficiency of the construction process. The review of the design, bid and contract documents for constructability should also include specific elements of the sustainability program for most cost efficient installation and availability of materials.

3.1.4 Cost control

During the design process the CM develops and maintains cost control procedures to monitor and control project expenditures, both current and projected, within the allocated budget. Sustainable projects statistically have relatively elevated capital – or "first" – costs, often offset by lower life cycle costs. In order to properly assess the costs of a project with specifically identified sustainability goals, objectives and requirements, several analyses may be required to align goals and requirements with budgets and schedules.

Alternative studies

Alternatives analysis is a standard practice used to identify alternative means to achieve specified project objectives. Alternatives analysis is more effective and efficient when undertaken early in a project life cycle.

A project may be found to have competing strategies to achieve sustainability objectives. Multi-criteria analysis (MCA) is a valuable and increasingly widely-used tool to aid decision-making where there are competing options, and particularly useful as a tool for sustainability assessment where a complex and inter-connected range of environmental, social and economic issues must be taken into consideration and where objectives are competing, make trade-offs unavoidable. MCA can be applied at all levels of decision-making, from the consideration of project alternatives to broad-reaching policy decisions guiding a transition toward sustainability and the green economy.

MCA and similar complex alternatives analyses may require facilitation by an experienced consultant. This need should be identified early and anticipated by the budget and design process.

Life Cycle Analysis (LCA)

The goal of LCA is to compare environmental and social damages assignable to products and services so as to choose the least burdensome options. The term "life cycle" refers to the notion that a fair, holistic assessment requires the assessment of raw material production, manufacture, distribution, use and disposal including all intervening transportation steps necessary or caused by the product's existence. The sum of these steps is the life cycle of the product. The concept can be used to optimize the environmental performance of a single product or an entire project. Life Cycle Assessment is carried out in four distinct phases:

- Establishment of goal and scope;
- Life cycle inventory;
- Life cycle impact assessment; and
- Interpretation.

Like alternatives analysis for sustainability projects, LCA may require an experienced facilitator, which must be identified early in order to anticipate budget requirements and retain a reliable service provider capable of providing input in a timely fashion.

References:
- International Organization for Standardization: http://www.iso.org/iso/catalogue_detail?csnumber=37456
- U.S. EPA: http://www.epa.gov/nrmrl/lcaccess/

Energy modeling
Energy modeling or simulation models heating, cooling, lighting, ventilating, and other energy flows as well as water in buildings.

LEED requires energy modeling if any of the 10 points possible under Energy & Atmosphere Credit 1, for optimizing energy performance, are to be attained.

Numerous programs are available for purchase. The U.S Department of Energy offers a number of programs free of charge.

Responsibility for energy modeling and simulation should be assigned to the A/E. Energy analyses should be conducted by the A/E team frequently enough to validate the design solution.

Responsibility for realizing energy performance results differs depending on the contracting strategy, and must be addressed in contractual instruments.

Risk assessment
The cost, schedule, technical feasibility and other risks on a project with sustainability goals, objectives and requirements may be heightened by uncertainties related to experience in the design and construction team, performance of unique design, solutions, equipment or means and methods.

Risk management seeks to minimize uncertainty regarding future events. Risk assessment is a tool to predict the likelihood of future events and the effects of these future events. Risk mitigation manages risk proactively based on the outcome of risk assessment. In using risk assessment and mitigation techniques, the project team should take care to assure sustainability features and goals are protected and conserved as critical project elements to be protected and conserved throughout the design and construction process.

Value engineering, value analysis, alternatives
Value engineering (VE) is a systematic method designed to improve the value of a project through examination of cost saving proposals or functional improvements that increase the ratio of function to cost. A primary tenet of value engineering is that basic functions of a project must be preserved - not reduced – as a consequence of value engineering. A key responsibility of the CM is to assure that the sustainability features of a project are not sacrificed during the course of VE efforts in design or construction.

Sustainable development, design and construction processes by definition seek to reverse the trend that focuses on facility first costs and undervalues or excludes consideration of the operational costs of a facility, which in terms of energy, can involve significant investment. Defining the project budget for the purpose of the VE exercise involves identifying the cost of the facility over its entire life cycle, including first costs, costs of replacements and alterations, and operations and maintenance, which in most cases is by far the most costly stage of a facility's useful life. VE is thus well-suited as a tool to assist in achieving sustainability objectives.

The risk of VE to sustainability arises when there are real or perceived additional costs associated with sustainability features that are not clearly identified as functional requirements. Clearly articulated energy efficiency goals are effective insurance against VE exercises that eliminate sustainability features.

Not all sustainable concepts yield the best results at the lowest costs. This is very evident in the USGBC LEED Process where the capturing of many points adds none to very little cost to the project while others will generate a major premium to secure. Trade-off studies are a traditional part of value engineering and time must be allotted in the schedule to study the sustainable approach in terms of good value of costs and effectiveness meeting sustainability goals. It is especially important to undertake this effort at the schematic design stage, when it is most appropriate to adjust the scope of the project with least impact to the schedule.

Project estimates

The responsibility for the preparation and maintenance of the project cost estimates should belong to the CM. Projects with sustainability requirements may involve technologies with limited pricing and installation information. Due care should be afforded to develop adequate contingencies in these cases.

3.1.5 Commissioning

During design, the owner's project sustainability requirements are translated into construction documents. Design phase commissioning objectives include verifying that the owner's sustainability requirements are captured in the basis of design documents that articulate the design intent and scope, assuring that that design processes are leveraged to include commissioning requirements in construction documents, identifying training and acceptance requirements, and performance of commissioning-focused design review.

Contractor responsibilities for commissioning are defined in the commissioning specifications that must be coordinated with other commissioning team members when planning the commissioning process. The CA assumes the lead role with the design team in developing the commissioning specification. The CA details the roles and responsibilities of the contractors in the commissioning process throughout the project. A draft set of system readiness checklists and verification test procedures should be included in the commissioning specification to communicate to the bidding contractor the sustainability requirements to be verified and the level of rigor that is expected during the testing phase of commissioning.

4.0 Procurement Phase

4.1 Introduction

The goal of this phase is to conduct the procurement process in a manner that will comply with sustainability goals, objectives and requirements, secure service providers and suppliers capable of satisfying the contract documents, and result in the successful and timely award of contracts for construction.

Sustainability in the procurement phase will have limited effect on the schedule, though an added layer of complexity in the contract documents may result in a larger number of bid questions, which may lead to larger or additional addenda. The design and CM team's experience in resolving bid issues related to sustainable work scopes should be factored in to bidding, bid evaluation and award durations.

4.1.1 Procurement planning

Sustainability is identified in the Project or Construction Management Plan. Sustainability goals, objectives and requirements are incorporated by design into the contract documents as design evolves. The CM should assure that the master schedule assures adequate time for procurement provisions and market conditions related to sustainability, specifically for advertisement, bid and award, together with any special approvals during the award cycle.

4.1.2 Advertisement and solicitation of bids

The requirements for project sustainability features and measures such as LEED certification requirements and energy performance requirements must be clearly presented in the advertisement and solicitation for bids. Language might include:

- Design Services: "Provide evidence of experience in sustainability design practices. Identify experience in using an integrated design approach, life cycle assessment, life cycle cost analysis, LEED and other practices used by your firm in meeting sustainable design goals. Identify participating team members with appropriate experience on a project with similar sustainability measures. Provide evidence of LEED accreditation."

- Construction: "Provide evidence of experience in implementing sustainability and or LEED during construction. Identify experience in implementing C&D waste management and on-site recycling programs, use of sustainable materials with high recycle content, use of low-emitting materials, use of air monitoring, efficient use of equipment and utilities energy during construction, commissioning and documentation of sustainability and LEED. Identify the participating construction site team members responsible for and with appropriate experience with sustainability and LEED implementation. Demonstrate an understanding of the integrated nature of the design relative to sustainability. Provide evidence of experience with the process of evaluating the impact of changes not only in regard to cost but also on the building's intended operation. Show that proposed team members have a thorough understanding of the concept of life cycle analysis. Provide evidence of personnel and craft training in sustainability and or LEED implementation including documentation."

The CM should participate in all pre-bid meetings, site visits, and addenda preparation to clarify features of the project that are associated with sustainability goals, objectives and requirements.

4.1.3 Select bidders list

Many owners, if permitted by applicable bidding laws and regulations, may identify and pre-qualify bidders they believe are qualified to pursue work in their market. The CM should assist the owner in managing any prequalification steps or establishing appropriate standards prior to advertisements for bids. The CM should verify by reference checks that the pre-qualified bidders have a track record of practicing sustainability and/or have experience implementing project with sustainability requirements.

4.1.4 Instructions to Bidders

The Instructions to Bidders section of a solicitation should be comprehensive and include clear, concise information to complement the advertisement or solicitation statement. The CM should review instructions to bidders so that sustainability requirements are reasonably reflected by the document. Instructions should advise the bidders of the procedures and requirements for submitting an acceptable proposal for the owner's review. Language might include:

- Design Services: "Demonstrated experience in sustainable design practices is mandatory. Identify experience in using an integrated design approach, life cycle cost analysis, and other practices used by your firm in meeting sustainable design goals. Identify participating team members with appropriate experience.

- Construction: "Demonstrated experience in sustainable project construction practices is mandatory. Identify experience in implementing the construction of projects with sustainable design requirements. Identify participating construction team members with appropriate experience."

4.1.5 Pre-bid conference

A pre-bid conference should be held involving all design or construction or design/build contracts being solicited by an owner. In addition to pertinent scope of work, schedule information, and important contract terms, the CM should outline the sustainability and or LEED certification and experience requirements for the project.

4.1.6 Proposal document protocol and proposal/bid opening

The CM and owners team should review each proposal/bid to determine which proposer/bidder has appropriate sustainability experience. The proposer/bidder is ranked and the sustainability ranking score is considered when completing the overall proposer/bidder selection.

4.1.7 Pre-award conference/scope review meeting

The owner and CM should conduct a pre-award conference with the apparent successful bidder to review and discuss the terms, conditions, costs and scope of work including sustainability requirements. The conference could be a personal meeting with the parties, or via telephone, depending on the issues involved and should be structured to assure all parties have clear understanding of the contract and scope of sustainable design and implementation during the construction phase of the project. This is the opportunity to find out first hand how the designer or contractor plans to implement sustainability for the project. It is also an opportunity to assess how well the designer or contractor will become a true partner in the project.

4.1.8 Contract award

The owner or CM should formally notify successful bidder by letter that they have been identified as most responsive bidder for a contract that has specific sustainability requirements.

5.0 Construction Phase

5.1 Introduction

The goal of this phase is to complete the construction in accordance with the requirements of the contract documents, applicable codes and regulations, and the sustainability goals, objectives and requirements have been embedded in the contract documents.

5.1.1 Contractor QA/QC

The contractor achieves construction quality by utilizing the specified materials to build the specified project, using competent craft persons to install the materials, and implementing a formal construction quality control program. The program should be a written document, termed the QC program, which includes procedures (or instructions) and controls that adequately address the type of work required by the contract document. A project's sustainability requirements are embedded in the contract documents. Thus, the QC program by definition should articulate the procedures and controls for achieving quality implementation of the features that render a project "sustainable."

If the contractor is required to provide inspection and testing services, the contractor should include a list of testing consultants in the QC program, along with credentials and certifications for each.

Construction Management Plan
The Project/Construction Management Plan should be updated to reflect the GC team makeup and roles and responsibilities for tasks specifically associated with project sustainability requirements, such as C&D waste management, recycling, suppliers, commissioning activities, etc.

Project procedures
The Project Procedures Manual should be updated to include contractor work plans and submittal requirements related to the sustainability goals, objectives and requirements of the project, such as:

- C&D waste management plans;
- Recycling plans;
- Construction phase indoor air quality provisions and procedures;
- Material certifications and documentation; and
- Commissioning or Acceptance Testing.

Commissioning plan schedule

The CM and CA should work closely with the GC to integrate commissioning activities into the overall construction schedule, keep commissioning activities off the critical path, and schedule site inspections that focus on systems operations and maintenance. The commissioning schedule is developed as a section of the Commissioning Plan and is updated throughout the project. Detailed integration of commissioning activities and tasks with the construction schedule is critical to maintaining project milestones and verifying that sustainability requirements are met.

5.1.2 Pre-construction conference

The pre-construction conference should include a detailed discussion of the project's sustainability goals, objectives and requirements, particularly if LEED or Green Globes targets are anticipated. The GC or designated "lead contractor" should be asked to present a plan designed to achieve these objectives, and an overview of sustainable construction practices that will be employed.

The CM should review roles and responsibilities during the construction phase. Personnel from each firm (A/E, CM, contractor, owner and others if applicable) should be designated as responsible for the LEED/Green Globe effort and compliance.

The CM should review specific RFI expectations, particularly if they are to be submitted to the USGC or GBI for review and comment.

The CM should review documentation submittal expectations such as:

- LEED letter templates;
- Waste manifest detail;
- Local suppliers detail; and
- Recycled material detail.

The CM should review expected sustainable practices on site, such as:

- Deconstruction vs. demolition;
- Waste Management Plan;
- Material reuse;
- No idling;
- Noise mitigation;
- Minimal waste;
- No smoking; and
- Office (minimize paper usage – electronic media; double sided printing where necessary; maximize power usage efficiencies; etc.

The CM must be aware of various elements in the project requiring special operations control including sustainability elements particularly if the project is identified for LEED certification. These elements may be related to heavy construction field activities as well as those associated with manufacturing facilities, treatment plants, operations control centers, and other facilities dealing with instrumentation and control systems or other as required by contract. To provide for an acceptable level of quality in the project for these facilities, the CM should review the specification requirements for the work with the contractor to confirm that the contractor and its suppliers are focused on quality and the specific requirements as noted by contract. Attention should be paid to the impact on the environment and any sustainable requirements. They should recognize the need to install these elements in the completed project in a manner that allows them to be utilized for their intended purpose.

5.1.3 Construction planning and scheduling

The contractor must submit a realistic work plan and CPM schedule that conforms to the contract's requirements. The schedule duration must include sufficient time to produce quality work and include time for submission, approval, procurement, testing, commissioning, inspection and verification. The CM should also coordinate with the owner and designer to make them aware of their responsibilities in supporting the project schedule.

The schedule submitted by the contractor should include activities related to sustainability, and should anticipate additional material lead time requirements or extended construction durations. For example, adaptive reuse of building and components and reusing existing materials will add a level of complexity to construction. Securing products from a regional source may place limitations on material sourcing that can impact the schedule as certain sustainable products may prove to have a longer lead period for acquisition and longer installation periods than more familiar products.

While equipment start-up is technically part of commissioning, it can often occur well before the project completion and must be coordinated with the design engineering and commissioning team. Advanced commissioning for LEED and other programs may also call for other interim inspections, test and documentation submittals that must be coordinated with the construction schedule.

While start-up is generally a milestone or a short duration activity, commissioning periods should be ample to allow for a complete battery of testing, training and documentation before occupancy. The program task of commissioning for each major component should appear both on the Construction Schedule and the Master Schedules to remind all that it is an important and time sensitive part of the development process. The Commissioning Agent should review and provide insight into duration and logic of these activities. Too often, projects are scheduled for occupancy at Substantial Completion without adequate consideration for commissioning, when pre-planning for commissioning would have yielded a better product at occupancy.

If one of the goals of the project were to achieve a certain level of sustainability, such as LEED, the schedule should include an activity with a duration reflecting the time needed between final assembly of documentation and receipt of the award decision from USGBC. This could take up to a year or longer after the final application is submitted. The owner should be made aware of this timeframe in order to align expectations with reality.

5.1.4 Construction Management and administration

Sustainability checklist (status reports)
The sustainability checklist or scorecard, which was included in contract documents, should be actively leveraged by the GC to monitor status and progress of work elements that are integral to project sustainability objectives.

Changes in work
Change management procedures should clearly identify a rigorous scope review process and approval authorities that avoids changes in construction that compromise sustainability goals, objectives and requirements. This can be accomplished through a change review board, panel, or process that includes the A/E and CA in a review capacity.

The contract documents set forth specific requirements to document and obtain approval by the owner of any changes in the work. The contractor's QA/QC program should outline the procedures that staff must follow when changes occur. The CM is routinely charged with the responsibility to evaluate any changes, deletions or additions to the work under the contract as to its effect on construction time, cost and quality.

The CM or GBF should confirm what impact any proposed change orders on the project have on the targeted sustainability goals, objectives and requirements, particularly for projects targeting LEED certification. Any impact should be communicated in writing to the project team with the objective of soliciting alternative solutions that don't negatively impact the targeting sustainability measures, keeping in mind the project budget and schedule. All executed change orders, and backup documentation that affect the targeted sustainability measures level should be compiled by the CM or GBF throughout the project for submission to the appropriate authorities.

Document control and distribution
Procedures for document routing and management should be clearly identified in the Project and Construction Management Plan to alert all parties to project status, progress and requirements.

When the contractor performs work without using the current applicable design, the contractor is at risk for the work's not being accepted. The CM should review, or audit, the contract document control section of the contractor's QA/QC manual to determine if the program is in conformance. The audit should include a check of document holders at the construction site to determine that they have and are using the latest drawings, specifications and other appropriate information.

The USGBC documentation requirements for LEED certification are strict, which makes proper documentation control and distribution important. The firm responsible for the LEED certification, along with key designated team members, must receive all current documents in a timely manner. Document control and distribution procedures should include requirements regarding distribution to the firm responsible for the LEED certification.

Requests for Information (RFIs)
RFIs should be routed by the CM to the CA, the GBF as well as to the A/E so that clarification and direction to the contractor reflects measures to conserve sustainability features of the project. The relationship of any project element to the sustainability program may not be readily apparent to some project participants. The integrated team must be alerted by way of standard document processing.

Non-conforming and corrective work
Non-conforming and corrective work has the potential to negatively impact facility performance as well as the targeted sustainability or LEED certification. The project team, including the CM, has the responsibility to verify that non-conforming work is corrected and deviations from the contract documents should be properly documented. This documentation should be included in the LEED certification submission package where required.

QC inspection and testing documentation
Most government agencies and many major corporations have detailed procedures designating the inspections and tests required for their projects. As a minimum, the contractor's QA/QC program must include provisions to confirm that specified inspections and tests occur at the appropriate times during the construction process. The CM should confirm that the inspections and tests are in accordance with the contract specifications, including any sustainability requirements.

The CM must verify that the contractor's QC program adequately addresses the requirement to ensure that the products submitted and approved are the products utilized on site. Attention to detail is paramount as products sometimes viewed as the least critical are the most important when VOC limits are concerned. Such products include but are not limited to PVC glues, construction adhesives, primers/sealers, glues for finish installation and paints/coatings.

The CM should review the contract documents for indications that appropriate test and measurement devices are identified, properly calibrated and properly used. The CM should also review contractors' procedures by auditing to observe that the program is being satisfactorily implemented.

The CM should ask the Commissioning Agent and other consultants and contractors responsible for testing and monitoring to verify utility and calibration of testing instruments.

Sustainability quality audits

An audit of sustainability requirements can be used to verify that quality management systems are in place so as to achieve sustainability requirements. Typically, the contractor provides quality control, while the CM or a selected independent agency provides quality assurance oversight on the project. Under a sustainable project, much of this QA function may be provided under the GBF or CA.

Commissioning

During construction, commissioning activities are vital to verifying that sustainability goals are met. These include updating the owner's project requirements to reflect changes made in the procurement period, updating the Commissioning Plan to include new or revised elements introduced throughout the construction process; development and distribution of testing and inspection procedures; performance of testing and inspection activities; documentation of testing and inspection activities; integration of commissioning activities in the construction schedule; verify development of systems and training manuals, and provision of commissioning reports and training requirements pursuant to the Commissioning Plan.

Project documentation

When a project is to be LEED certified, some party should be contractually bound to organize LEED supporting documentation, whether it is the CM, the CA or the GBF. The CM should make this requirement known to the GC as early as possible in the project. Documentation should not be compiled at close-out, but should be ongoing throughout submittal, procurement, and construction of the work. The CM should institute a system for gathering documentation from the beginning of construction and continue throughout the project.

A thorough system of documenting sustainability measures should be maintained by the appropriate parties throughout construction. Documentation procedures should specify the collection of documentation related to such items as waste management and recycling, emissions mitigations, noise and vibrations mitigations, dust reduction efforts, and proper materials storage and handling. (The CM should note, for example, when ductwork is installed that it is capped until permanently terminated; documentation should show if sheetrock has been stored properly such that it is properly protected from moisture, which could foster mold.)

If an independent CA is to be employed by the CM related documentation should be compiled by the CA throughout the life of the project most notably during the construction phase. If an independent

49

CA is employed by the owner, the CM should report to the owner if the CA, in the CM's judgment, is not furnishing the appropriate paperwork in a timely manner.

Progress payments
The CM should only approve requests for payment for accepted materials/items or completed and accepted construction, unless contract documents provide otherwise. The progress payment process should include any sustainability requirements. The contractor should include in their schedule of values a line item for these requirements, and should be paid a percentage as progress is made.

Payments for sustainable equipment and installations may be tied to the contractor providing the proper sustainable documentation for that equipment and installation, to ensure that the documentation is kept current.

When the contractor has specific obligations to meet certain sustainability goals such as LEED gold etc., schedule of values must identify the value and sufficient funds must be withheld until the sustainability goal is achieved.

Acceptance testing
When a full commissioning program is not justified, specific pieces of equipment or systems can be subject to "acceptance testing" for purposes of owner acceptance. This abbreviated form of commissioning can also be used to verify achievement of certain sustainability goals or requirements. The CM or other assigned party develops the test procedures and acceptance criteria to very that equipment or systems meet performance criteria. The tests are normally conducted using contractor personnel and witnessed by the CM and/or owner. Training of owner personnel in operation and maintenance is part of the acceptance test. Each element of the test procedure is implemented and signed off when found to meet the criteria. The CM verifies that all tests have been satisfactory completed, before final acceptance.

Beneficial occupancy/substantial completion
As the project approaches beneficial occupancy/substantial completion, the construction quality program should include reviews of incomplete work, corrective actions to remedy nonconformance and other quality requirements including documentation. Reviews should include sustainability requirements.

The CM should not recommend beneficial occupancy to the owner until the project punch list is prepared by the contractor, and accepted by the CM and owner, and all areas are available for use. If the project is to be LEED certified or similar, all open review comments related to sustainability features should be included.

This may be particularly difficult for a CM-at-Risk that may be under pressure to secure a Substantial Completion Certificate in order to facilitate occupancy in accordance with contractual deadlines. The CM-at-Risk and owner should be mindful that punch list activities following owner occupancy often result in disputes requiring differentiation of punch list work from damage or changed conditions due to the owner's use of the property.

Training

Within a reasonable period of training, some nominal percentage of trainees should be randomly selected and tested or informally evaluated on the material covered in the program, with the objective of verifying that trainees are being provided with pertinent information required to operate and maintain the facility per the owner's requirements, and maximize the project's sustainability features.

Providing the Facility Management staff with digital records of the training sessions may significantly increase the value of the training by providing the staff with a reference for future post-occupancy training of new personnel, as well as for future reference of the staff for procedures that may not be used frequently.

Substantial completion

The contract documents should articulate the conditions required to meet this milestone with respect to a project's sustainability features. The CM should review the contract and completed work to record that the contractor has attained this milestone as defined by the contract and make appropriate recommendations to the owner. The owner and design professional should concur that the milestone has been reached. Minor punch list work not affecting the use of the facility by the owner may remain incomplete with the approval of the owner and CM for substantial completion.

Final acceptance

Final acceptance follows Substantial Completion and the completion of punch list work, with the concurrence of the A/E, the CM and the CA. If final acceptance is to precede final certification by USGBC or other sustainable certification process, this should be clearly articulated in the contract documents.

Typically, all punch list work has been completed to the satisfaction of the owner, A/E, CM, and CA prior to Final Acceptance (and associated payment) to the satisfaction of the owner, A/E, CM, and CA. A project with sustainable certification requirements may have a few activities that must be completed many months past the completion of typical punch-list work, such as "off season" commissioning or receipt of notification of the final USGBC certification. This dynamic can be addressed contractually by creating items in the schedule of values associated with such late-breaking requirements.

6.0 Post-Construction Phase

6.1.1 Post-construction checklist

LEED measurement, verification and certification

During the post-construction phase, the CM's responsibility is to identify and expedite the submittal of documentation necessary and/or required by the contract. The LEED application will be submitted by the party designated as the LEED agent for the project. This could be the CM, A/E, the GBF, or CA. Responsibility for these tasks should be identified in contract documents and project management plans.

Upon receipt of the preliminary LEED Review document noting the credit achievement anticipated, pending, and denied. In addition, up to six (6) prerequisites and/or credits will be selected for audit. The project team will have 25 business days to provide corrections and additional supporting documents as a supplementary submittal to the application.

Upon receipt of the Final LEED Review, the project team has 25 business days to notify the USGBC that they accept the Final LEED Review or that they will appeal the rating. If no appeal is submitted, the project will then be certified subject to the USGBC's Final Review.

The CM should advise the client that implementation of the professional standards for quality building environments used during the construction phase should continue during the building's operational phase. These standards include, but are not limited to:

1. Maintaining a well qualified building operations staff and training them on how to use and maintain all equipment.
2. Establishing procedures for inspection, preventive maintenance, cleaning, and repair of all equipment.
3. Creating and maintaining a resource center for purchase of additional equipment and maintenance stock that comes from sustainable sources.
4. Reading and becoming familiar with the Material Safety Data Sheets (MSDS) on cleaning chemicals and pesticides, and avoid using products that may release harmful chemicals into the air.
5. Recycling waste materials.
6. Setting up a call center to log tenant complaints and follow-up on these. Problems that are identified early may cost less to fix now than later.
7. Continuing to monitor indoor air quality for compliance with the latest guidelines.
8. Adjusting light levels for use of space and occupancy.
9. Using LEED standards during any building renovation projects.

10. Requiring LEED standards to be used during any move into or move out of the facility.

6.1.2 Commissioning

Commissioning in the post-construction phase begins at substantial completion. At a minimum, commissioning activities should continue through the end of the contractual warranty/correction period and ideally continue throughout the life of the facility. During this period, the ongoing operation, maintenance and modification of facility systems and assemblies, and associated documentation, are verified against updated owner project requirements, including sustainability requirements.

6.1.3 Re-commissioning or continuous commissioning

The performance of dynamic systems and equipment, as well as static systems, assemblies and components, will tend to degrade from as-installed condition over time. In addition, the needs and demands of facility users and processes typically change during the course of a facility's use. Maintaining the sustainability features of a project may require periodic evaluation and adjustment. The continuous commissioning – or re-commissioning – process has the main objectives of assuring that an owner's project requirements reflect changes in use and operation of the facility; periodic evaluation performance against the owner's project objectives; maintaining the system manual to reflect changes in the owner's project requirements, and ongoing training of operations and maintenance personnel and occupants on current owners requirements and changes in systems and assemblies.

6.1.4 Retro-commissioning

When an owner adopts commissioning on a project during the operation stage of the facility life cycle, then commissioning is termed "Retro-Commissioning" and, while it accomplishes commissioning process activities, it is sufficiently different from the commissioning as otherwise depicted in this document that it is considered a separate process.

Improvements in major energy consuming features such as HVAC systems, lighting and communications are happening at increasing speeds. "State of the art" five years ago may now be obsolete. Retro-Commissioning of a five or 10-year-old building, along with updating of equipment or components may result in a substantial reduction in energy use. This may incentivize an owner to revisit commissioning frequently.

Please consult ASHRAE Guideline 0-2005 for further information.

6.1.5 Asset/facilities management – Life cycle monitoring

Technology is progressing at an incredible rate. Five-year-old fluorescent light tubes and fixtures may be energy wasters compared to current technologies. Such developments may dramatically alter a Life Cycle Analysis after a few years. Monitoring efficiency improvements of building components can be worthwhile.

6.1.6 Training

Training of the owner's operation and maintenance staff occurs ideally during construction. Some training, however, is best deferred until the owner has assumed responsibility for the sustainability features. Such training should be identified in the Commissioning Plan. Training should clearly define maintenance required for continued function of sustainability features.

6.1.7 Seasonal commissioning

Seasonal commissioning pertains to testing under full-load conditions during peak heating and peak cooling seasons, as well as partial load conditions in the spring and fall. Whereas initial commissioning is done as soon as contract work is completed irrespective of the season, seasonal conditioning requires testing of equipment and systems in a peak season to observe peak load performance, in which heating equipment is tested during winter extremes and cooling equipment is tested during summer extremes with a fully occupied building. Construction contracts should specify contractor participation in seasonal commissioning to realize and or verify achievement of sustainability goals.

6.1.8 Operation and maintenance/owner's maintenance vs. warranty call-back

The CM may find it difficult to get an owner to accept that the facility management staff needs to take "ownership" of the new facility. Owners may feel that a specific issue is warranty-related, while contractors may argue that it should be considered to be an owner's maintenance issue.

Carefully define obligations on both sides in the bid documents, clearly stating the owner's maintenance obligations following occupancy. While the contractor may be obligated to provide a full year warranty, the owner's construction cost at bid time may be more favorable if bid documents clearly state that, upon Substantial Completion, the owner will be responsible for such things as changing failed light bulbs, replacing clogged filters and worn belts, and adjusting door hardware. Contractors may also more favorably perceive bid documents that limit attic stock for maintenance purposes to a specified amount of customary items such as ceiling tiles, floor coverings, and wall coverings during a warranty period.

6.1.9 Warranty call-back program/owner's contact info. for responsible parties

Contractors should be required to provide the owner, in close-out submittals, with the names of qualified individuals to be contacted in the event of a warranty-related problem during the warranty period.

For equipment or other building component that are critical to the operation of the building, designated contacts should be reachable on-call. Many building management systems are externally monitored by an independent third party, and these firms should also be provided with the names and contact information of the various contractors whose work is under their monitoring efforts.

The owner should provide a similar point of contact, available 24 hours per day, to enable a contractor may to enter the facility to rapidly correct or mitigate a problem and avert potential environmental damage and minimize waste.

6.1.10 Deconstruction

At the end of the building's useful life, the owner should identify potential re-use for the building components. This could include structural components, furniture, and recyclable materials. Through thoughtful deconstruction, the owner will minimize the building's contribution to landfill waste, and continue to contribute to sustainable construction projects.

Index

O

Off-the-grid · 9

P

Project management · 9, 12, 13, 14, 15, 17, 24, 29, 32, 52
Project Safety Plan · 13

Q

Quality Management Plan · 13, 16

R

Rainwater harvesting · 9
Renewable energy · 2, 9, 12
Renewable Energy Credits · 9
Retro-Commissioning · 10, 53,
Risk management · 19, 20, 21, 29, 39

S

Safety · 4, 12, 13, 19, 20, 52
Sustainability Plan · 11, 12, 17, 23, 24, 29, 30
Sustainable development · 10, 18, 33, 39

Sustainable Forestry Initiative (SFI) · 14
Sustainable materials · 10, 11, 41

T

Time management · 15
Transparency · 11

U

U.S. Green Building Council (USGBC) · 7, 8, 11, 14, 19, 27, 36, 40, 47, 48, 51, 52

V

Value engineering · 17, 33, 39, 40
Volatile organic compounds · 11

W

Waste management · 3, 5, 8, 9, 31, 36, 41, 44, 45, 49

Z

Zero-energy building · 9, 11